# Tate McRae
# The Ultimate Guide

## Updated Edition

Megan Stallwood

# Contents

# Introduction

Tate McRae is a Canadian singer, songwriter and dancer. She has already had a great dancing career winning awards, appearing on television and working with famous musicians. Her YouTube channel has had over a billion views, and her songs are extremely popular - especially among her large loyal fanbase.

Tate is now becoming a big star with her music and style. Her debut album released in 2022 has gained positive reviews. Find out more about Tate and her career in this book: Tate McRae The Ultimate Guide.

*This book was originally released in 2021. This is the expanded and updated edition.*

# Tate

Tate's song You released in 2021 broke the record for the fastest song to reach number one on the Billboard Dance/Airplay chart.

-

Tate started dancing at the age of 6. She started competing in dance competitions at the age of 8.

-

In March 2021 Tate received two Juno Award nominations.

These were for Breakthrough Artist and the Fan Choice Award.

-

Tate's favourite comfort food? Toast.

-

On May 8 2021 Tate performed in a global virtual concert. The concert was titled "Too Young to Be Sad".

Along with Tate were a two piece band and background dancers. The show included "poetic interludes" from Tate.

Ali Shutler from the New Musical Express website thought it was "slick, impressive, thoughtful and a constant spectacle with pop star ambition."

-

Tate graduated from High School in January 2021.

-

Tate and Khalid's single Working got the support of 124 Mediabase monitored stations.

-

Tate thought that headlining her own sell out tour was something that would never happen.

-

It has been said that Tate was "built for Tik Tok" because of her dancing skills and her emotional ballads.

-

Tate said of Tik Tok:

"It's literally the main source of what teenagers are thinking about every single day," she says.

"It feels like a huge group chat where everyone comes together and sees the same things, and thinks the same way. So it's important to be on it and, obviously, make your songs go on there."

-

Tate likes dark chocolate.

-

Tate said of social media:

"Sometimes I actually forget that I'm a public figure and that everyone watching can form their own opinions on me without actually meeting me. It's the craziest feeling," she says.

Recently, she says, she's started shutting off her social accounts "as much as I can, to maintain my own life". Instead, she wants to communicate through her lyrics.

"I like to be as vulnerable as I can in my music so that fans can really get to know what's inside my brain," she says.

-

Tate says she is the worst at giving titles to her songs.

-

Tate says a dream duet would be with Post Malone.

-

Tate says she wants to change the world by making meaningful music.

-

Tate says her dream dinner party guests would be Leonardo DiCaprio, Timothée Chalamet, and Zendaya.

-

Tate says her biggest fear is losing someone she loves.

-

Tate says that at school she was not a rebel - but was not a teacher's pet either!

-

When Tate was younger she went to perform in Dubai on a glass floor - only to realise it was a pool of water!

-

Tate says she has never been banned from anywhere!

-

Tate says she has a car and a moon as her phone background.

-

Sony made a special immersive experience featuring Tate performing in 3D. It uses Spatial Reality Display so viewers do not need to use 3D glasses to watch.

The experience uses effects powered by the Unreal engine and shows Tate's history to become a popular artist.

A dance routine by Tate for her song You

Broke Me first is also included. This is a part of Sony's Collaboration Series where music artists are connected with Sony technology, movies and gaming and to showcase the new Spatial Reality Display technology.

The technology "follows the exact eye position of the viewer to create a highly realistic virtual and 3D experience that is viewable to the naked eye."

-

The cause Tate is most passionate about is mental health awareness.

-

Tate's favourite fictional character is Damon Salvatore.

He is a character from The Vampire Diaries TV show played by Ian Somerhalder

-

Tate says an item she cannot live without is an elastic band!

-

Tate is a fan of Gossip Girl.

-

Tate's favourite foods are Brussels Sprouts,
mashed potatoes and pizza.

-

Tate says she sets her alarm clock for 9 am.

-

Tate says the game show she would most like
to appear on is Family Feud.

-

One of Tate's ambitions is to perform at the
Superbowl.

-

Tate says her favorite time of the day is night
time - she is a night owl.

-

Tate says that when she younger she used to
talk to the ghost of her grandmother Omi.

-

Tate says she is not very punk - "0/10 punk!".

-

Tate prefers showers to baths.

-

Tate would like Zendaya to play her in a film.

"She's somebody that I have admired as a singer, dancer, and actor for a long time. I mean, everyone knows she's the coolest. "

-

Tate says she is obsessed with Christmas and that her favorite Christmas film is Elf.

-

Tate has an ambition to skydive.

-

In 2020, Tate was included in the Forbes 30 Under 30 List for 2021.

She was the youngest musician on the list.

\-

Tate says the first album she bought was "probably some sort of Disney soundtrack" as she was a fan of Camp Rock, High School Musical and Hannah Montana.

\-

Sony/ATV Creative Managers, Mya Hansen and Danielle Middleton had this to say about Tate:

"Watching Tate grow has been amazing – she has propelled her career in the midst of a global pandemic, all while finishing high school.

"We have no doubt that she is on her way to becoming a global superstar, and we are thrilled to be a part of her journey as a songwriter and artist."

\-

Tate says that she started to take her performing seriously when she started her YouTube channel aged 13.

\-

Tate says her song "One Day" posted on her

YouTube channel was her "first-ever breakout as a singer."

The song went viral and she got a deal with a music label as a result.

Calgary, Canada

Tate said that when when she was on the EMA's she was studying for her midterm.

"It's been really crazy over this entire experience because I'm still in high school...so, I'll be back and forth from writing an essay to doing an interview to filming an award show."

-

Tate's favourite breakfast?

Oatmeal with berries, or egg whites, cheese and turkey.

-

Tate said she first wanted to move from dance into music in 2018.

She said she fell in love with the whole process of the music industry - working in the studio and working with songwriters.

"The feeling of actually putting together a song is probably one of the best feelings ever".

-

Tate said she moved into music from dance because there was more freedom.

"You can take your vision and really bring it to life no matter what, because it's just you. You're not standing behind someone else or in a company where you have to follow really strict choreography. You basically have the final say."

But she still dances and her mom owns a

dance company!

-

The first record Tate bought was "I Kissed a Girl" by Katy Perry.

-

Tate says that when she was young she did not understand what songs were about, but just enjoyed the overall sound.

At some point she realised "Oh, damn, all my favourites are written about really specific things."!

-

Tate says as she has got older she listens to many different genres such as rap and R&B - different ones according to her mood.

In a 2020 interview she said she liked Post Malone, The Weeknd and Jessie Reyez.

-

Tate says that she does not suffer from stage fright when singing because she has been a professional dancer since the age of 8.

Singing is difficult from dancing because you have to sing and often you are the only person on the stage.

She said: " As a dancer, you get trained to carry on no matter what happens. You have to stay professional."

-

When Tate released her first single with RCA Tear Myself Apart it was the first time she was paid for her music.

"When you first get the paycheck, it's very rewarding, because you're doing something you love. It feels kind of unreal, because it doesn't feel like it's work."

-

Tate's first single Tear Myself Apart was written by Billie Eilish and Finneas O'Connell.

-

Tate says that she does not enjoy shopping for things like clothes at the mall for example.

Instead now and again she likes to buy something as a reward such as jewellery.

-

Tate is a big fan of the song Heather by Conan Gray as it is "very honest in its lyrics".

-

Tate said she is a fan of Mood by 24kGoldn and Iann Dior.

She said:

I'm not a rapper, but it's a pretty sick song. I sometimes wish that my alter ego was a rapper. It could happen one day. We'll see.

-

Tate said she met Justin Bieber when she was 12 and was starstruck.

She successfully auditioned as a dancer for his Purpose tour in 2016-17.

"I got to meet Justin backstage and then dance on stage with him. It was pretty damn cool. I was a big fan of JB."

-

Tate said on politics and the news:

"A lot of things that happen on the news every single day. The weird part is that with social media, you never know which line to cross or how much you should share. This world seems like a bit of a crazy mess right now. It's hard because there's so many things that go on and you can't really let it affect you anymore.

You just have to live your life.

There are so many things that are out of our hands. I'm 17, so I'm still forming my opinions and making sure that I know exactly what I believe in, and that's a hard thing to figure out sometimes."

-

Tate likes to keep her life private in case people misunderstand her words.

"I don't share anything on social media. As I'm getting older, I'm realising that you don't need to share your life online, because your words can get twisted into a million directions and your intentions never come across on text.

I think keeping your life private is the best way to go, while releasing your work and being vulnerable in that aspect of your life."

She does not like it when people make up

things about her "to hear someone make up a false accusation is one of the most stressful things in the world."

-

Tate says she is close to her mother and that they "have the closest relationship in the world".

-

Each week Tate uploaded an original song she had written on her YouTube channel.

Her song One Day became very popular and record label RCA signed Tate up.

-

In June 2021 Tate featured in a song by Blackbear called ul love u.

Blackbear is an American singer, musician, producer and songwriter.

The song is part of Blackbear's EP Misery Lake. U Love U has been described as a "poppy ballad".

Blackbear said of the song: "u love u is the

perfect blend of nostalgic synths and new school drums that paints a picture of what it's like to be in a relationship with a person who loves themselves so much that you feel alone.

Tate McRae then adds so much depth sonically to this song, it is truly a great way to start off the misery lake era of blackbear."

Tate said of the song: 'u love u' is a super honest song about the struggles of being in a relationship with a selfish person. I'm really excited to be a part of blackbear's record and help bring his vision to life."

Brussels Sprouts

1883 music said in an interview with Tate that interviewing her "feels just like you're hanging out with a younger sibling who you'd fight tooth and nail for".

-

After 1 month, Tate's debut EP All the Things I Never Said had had 53 million streams on Spotify.

-

Tate loves spending time with her fans at concerts as she feels they have helped her to become a star.

-

No creative decisions about Tate's career are taken without her consent.

She is in charge or her career.

-

In May Tate singed a deal to endorse water drink Essentia.

Essentia is an ionized, alkaline water that was invented by Ken Uptain in Seattle in 1998.

It was her first endorsement deal.

-

Tate enjoyed releasing her first work with a music company RCA as her 'YouTube songs were random whereas her EP was "a full story and a whole picture of who I am in the current moment".

-

For her EP All the Things I Never Said in 2020 Tate chose 5 songs from 35 she had written.

-

Tate says her songs are popular because they are personal stories and have a distinct story and are authentic.

They are not "just random words put into a melody and it doesn't really make sense to me and people will eventually be able to tell they aren't real, personal stories.....I can take all my songs and literally explain them each by each, letter by letter, and be able to tell exactly how I was feeling at that moment.".

-

Tate says she started songwriting as she loved poetry and writing at school.

-

Tate described herself in her younger days as "the kid who never shuts up!".

"Since I was 2, I've never stopped talking. I was one of those kids who started talking at a really abnormally young age, so my mom was like 'Gosh, she never stops talking!' I just always had stories to tell and I had the biggest imagination ever".

-

Variety said about Tate: "With a Lorde-like vocal pout, this 17-year-old Canadian delivers this song's sultry melody and spiralling chorus over a slinky trap beat ("don't be sad")".

-

Tate says she has never had and training in songwriting.

-

Tate says the music industry has changed as in the past record labels would find artists at concerts or auditions. Now they can find musicians on social media and YouTube.

"they're scouring through the Internet for hours upon hours every day. I don't even know what catches fire or what doesn't, it's just rapid content people are putting out and seeing what does well.".

-

Tate says she loves being Canadian and is proud to join "the ranks of Drake, Shawn Mendes, and other Canadian artists making it big in music".To know there are so many good Canadian artists out in the music industry now is really great. "

-

Tear Yourself Apart was the first song Tate released that she did not write. It was written by Billie Eilish,  Finneas O'Connell and  Eric Palmquist.

They thought the song would be good for Tate, and she said "I was obsessed with it. I put my own twist on it, and they really liked it. I'm such a big fan of all of them."

-

183 said about Tate:

"Tate McRae is laying down the groundwork to solidify herself as a deeply unique artist who can join the likes of other Gen-Z singers like Billie Eilish".

-

Tate said of her fans at her concerts: "They are my choir!"

-

On April 16, 2021 Tate released You.

Jason Lipshutz from Billboard magazine said that the song has "one of the most straightforward but delectable choruses of 2021.

-

Tate says fans were singing along to her songs a concerts before they were officially released - they found them on her YouTube channel.

-

In March 2021 Tate was named by Apple Music as an Up Next Artist.

This is monthly program by Apple to showcase rising talents. Every month an artist that Apple feel should have more promotion and attention is chosen by Apple.

Previous artists chosen include Billie Eilish Bad Bunny, Khalid and Sigrid.

-

Tate said about her fans at her concerts:

"The energy you get from them, staring up at you, is such a weird feeling you could never explain. Being on stage and knowing they are right there, full support, is something I never thought I would experience.".

-

Wonderland said about Tate:

"McRae's catchy bedroom pop is filled to the brim with propulsive rhythms, with her sharp undulating vocals drawing the listener in track after track."

-

Tate said of her fans:

"I love meeting them. They're the coolest fans ever, and I'm not even lying. Every time I meet them I'm like, damn I would be your friend.

You know, there are people you meet and you see how normal they are and it's easy to connect with them."

-

Tate enjoys bringing her dancing experience to her videos and performances.

"I have all of these dancers who are insane

and they are some of the best dancers right now, and they are some of my best friends.

It's been cool to translate it to my own music and be able to dance to my own lyrics and bring it to life.".

-

Ones to Watch said about Tate:

"Pop stars are getting younger and more talented by the day, and McRae is next in line."

-

Tate describes her hobbies as eating, hanging out with friends and watching Disney+.

-

Tate says dancing is an indescribable feeling.

"It can be the most frustrating thing in the world, but other times, nothing in the world could come close to it. It's a surreal feeling when you're just lost in it."

-

Tate is a fan of High School Musical: The Musical: The Series.

-

Tate says she is not too good at things other than music and dance as she does not have time!

"There's not much time for other things, so I suck at every other thing I do. I'm either good at things or terrible, there's no in - between. But I think I'm doing okay at music!"

-

Tate's mother and father are called Tanja and Todd.

She has an older brother called Tucker.

-

Tate's home city is Calgary in Canada.

-

Tate lived in the Middle East in Oman for a time when she was a child.

-

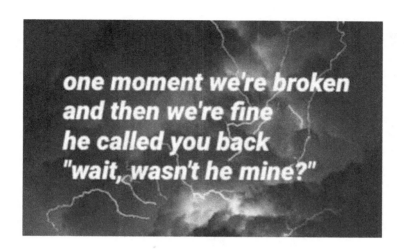

one moment we're broken
and then we're fine
he called you back
"wait, wasn't he mine?"

Tate's single Slower was released on March 3 2021.

-

Tate understands some German as her mother has a German background.

-

Wonderland said about Tate:

"McRae's catchy bedroom pop is filled to the brim with propulsive rhythms, with her sharp undulating vocals drawing the listener in track after track."

-

Tate attended Western Canada High School in Calgary.

-

Her work has got over a billion streams on Spotify.

-

Tate started her YouTube channel in 2011 concentrating on dance videos.

-

Tate was born on July 1st 2003. July 1st is Canada Day.

-

Tate says her generation can change the world by speaking up for themselves.

-

Tate's favourite style of dance in contemporary as she "likes to tell a story".

-

In April 2021 Tate signed a deal with CCS Rights Management.

The CCS Rights Management formed a new Neighbouring Rights Division which will manage Tate's recordings.

-

LadyGunn said about Tate:

"The ambitious queen never stops, thankfully for the rest of us, and her music is a reflection of her unrelenting hard work.

Using music to unravel and manage her emotions, Tate's been known to release song after song, connecting with her audience as often as she can."

-

Tate likes the fact that she is driven and motivated to do things.

"I'm a pretty self-motivated person and am a workhorse when under pressure."

-

Tate performed her first dance solo aged 8.

-

Her Campus said about Tate:

"Tate McRae brings an honest, vulnerable and emotional feeling to her music."

-

When she started dancing Tate would train up to 29 hours per week.

-

Tate's favourite movie is Footloose - the 2011 version starring Kenny Wormald.

-

Tate had an ambition to play the title role in Matilda the Musical on Broadway.

-

Tate had a crush on the character of Ian from the 2016 film Nerve. Ian is played by Dave Franco.

-

One of Tate's ambitions is to star in a

Hollywood movie.

-

Tate is able to work hard on her music as she is used to hard work and long hours through her dancing career.

"I'm so used to just grinding and working until it's done, As a dancer, you have this persistent energy that you are never going to leave your room until your work is finished."

-

Tate's full name is Tatum Rosner McRae.

-

Tate voiced a character in the Nickelodeon animated children's television series Lalaloopsy which ran from 2013-1015. Tate voiced the character of Spot Splatter Splash in 17 episodes.

-

TMRW said about Tate:

"Tate McRae has unsurprisingly won hearts and is well-worth all the attention".

-

When she was 4 years old Tate moved to the Middle Eastern state of Oman due to her father's work.

Her mother taught dance lessons in the country. She moved back to Calgary, Canada aged 8.

-

Tate said in 2020 that she thought Tiktok and social media had become the main source of distributing new music.

-

Tate said it was cool to see musicians finding new ways to engage with fans during the pandemic: "Many artists are actually making the most out of quarantine and creating music and music videos so I'm happy to see things are still going on."

-

Tate says she switched from dance related videos to music videos on her YouTube channel by accident.

"...one day the footage got messed up and I was like, 'Shoot!...I promised them I would post on Fridays! Let me just go in my bedroom. I was like, really mad, wrote this random song in 20 minutes and I was like, 'Here we're putting it online, My family hated it. I hated it. We were just like, 'O.K., put it out there.' Her music video went viral and got 30 million views.

-

Tate feels that social media and mobile phones have ruined dating and relationships. Tate said:

"I have this whole idea in my head that if phones didn't exist, social media didn't exist and this whole couldn't-care-less persona of every single person in the world didn't exist, that people would actually be able to find good love and not be in toxic relationships all the time.

People used to care so much more and put in so much effort and I feel like that's lacking so much nowadays, and it totally takes away from what a relationship is actually supposed to feel like."

-

Tate's manager said of her:

"She absolutely knows her brand, if you want to call it that, and none of us want to get in the way."

-

Tate's manager said she is similar to Billie Eilish as they are teenage artists making lyrically driven music. But they will have different styles of music.

-

Before the pandemic in 2020 Tate had only had six concerts.

-

Tate hopes to do some acting in the future but is concentrating on music at the moment.

-

11 record labels were looking to sign Tate. She went to New York with her parents to meet the labels.

Her father bought her a book  - Donald Passman's All You Need To Know About the

Music Business to help her decide. Tate said:

"I started to really look at artists' labels and how they [got their start]. It was, for the first time ever, when I started to look at [music] from a career point of view, like, 'How can I get myself into this industry?'"

-

Tate's father is a lawyer.

-

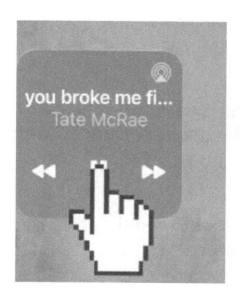

-

Elite Daily said about Tate:

"Not only is McRae an uber talented singer,

but she's got some serious moves."

-

Tate is a dog lover.

-

Tate said she once bought apple cider vinegar gummies off Instagram.

-

Tate has brown eyes.

-

Tate won the award for mini Best Dancer title of the 2013 version of Dance Award, New York

-

Tate won a silver medal during the New York Youth Grand Prix in 2015.

-

In 2015 Tate had intensive training scholarship with Berlin State Ballet School.

-

Tate appeared in So You Think You Can Dance: The Next Generation, the Fox tv show in 2016. she came 3rd and was the top female contestant.

-

Tate has mastered all main forms of dance.

-

NME music magazine said Tate is "...on a trajectory to become the newest pop idol."

-

Tate designs her own dancewear - she works with TWEAR dancewear.

-

Tate works with the YYC Dance Project based in Alberta, Canada.

-

Tate says that the song Small by Amanda Falk reminds her of childhood as her mom would play the song. Tate was a big fan of the song between 2 and 9!

-

In 2020 Tate was included on the Billboard 21 Under 21 To Watch List.

-

Tate says she has become a big fan of country music, mainly because her brother used to play the album What You See Is What You Get by Luke Combs on drives.

-

Tate is a fan of the song What a Time by Julia Michaels.

"She knows how to write songs like no other. She can really tap into my deep emotions and make me feel something. She's really captured how to put the feeling of love into words."

-

When the Party's Over by Billie Eilish is the song Tate plays when she is at her lowest.

-

Tate says that she finds it difficult to listen to some of her older YouTube songs.

"I've grown so much since then that it's hard to look back and really love them. "

-

Tate's favourite vegetable? Brussels Sprouts.

-

Somebody Else by The 1975 is the song Tate would choose if she could only hear one song for the rest of her life.

"It's my go-to driving song whenever I kinda feel like my world is falling apart."

-

Tate is a big fan of the The 1975.

-

The song which gets Tate "turned all the way up"? UCLA by RL Grime.

"There's something about this song that always gets everyone in the room hype".

-

Over It by Summer Walker is the album which

Tate wishes she had recorded.

"I've never skipped one song in this album. It's incredible."

-

Tate says Summer Walker is the coolest person ever.

-

Tate says that she will be happy to retire her song One Day.

"I wrote this when I was 13 and, for some reason, it still does super well. I love it, it's my baby, but it's gotta go hahah."

-

You Broke Me First is a song that Tate loves performing.

"It always makes me feel something, no matter how many times I perform it."

-

The media have described Tate as a bedroom pop idol. But she doesn't feel that label fits her style.

-

Tate describes her style as pop alternative, but "super focused on the lyrics".

"I don't go into a session thinking: I wanna write a pop song. It's like: I wanna write a new story today; I wanna bring that to life".

-

Tate says that many things inspire her songs: teenage emotions, friends, news stories...

"I feel like every single day, something new can inspire you and even when the least expected."

-

To create her songs Tate says she has an inspiration for a song, then freestyles with a guitar or piano, hones melodies then creates lyrics.

-

Tate enjoys songwriting, but does appreciate the views of other songwriters.

"....it's like seeing a whole other perspective on life when they start talking what they think of situations. At 17 years old I've got my ways and my opinions, but it's really cool to hear everyone else's."

-

Elle magazine called Tate "Canada's answer to Billie Eilish".

Tate said: I'm a big fan of Billie. For Elle to say that and I don't know, even just put me in that category that was crazy. I didn't expect that at all, and I'm very honoured."

-

Tate enjoyed her collaboration with Audrey Mika on SAYGRACE's Boys Ain't Shit.

"It's such a great message and song. We got into the studio with Grace. I recorded my verse, and we all met. It was a very fun and super cool process."

-

Tate wrote during the Pandemic in Canada. Her writers were in New York and LA, and they collaborated using Zoom.

"I've been just putting my head down, sitting in my room and getting a lot of stuff done." Tate said.

-

On her song Don't be Sad Tate said:

"It's not a love song. It's tackling my mental health at the time, how I was feeling inside and I'm really stoked."

-

Interns said about Tate:

"The honest lyrics are still there but they're joined by dark, moody beats. Her voice is smokey and instantly recognizable, sitting somewhere between Halsey and King Princess."

-

Tate says fans should have the freedom to interpret her songs so they see a reflection of themselves in them.

"I don't want people to feel like they're closed off to the only thing that they can think a song is about.

I want them to be able to interpret it into anything and feel like it could be their own thing that can help them through whatever they need to get through".

-

Tate loves You Broke Me First as she feels it is a timeless song that she can relate to herself.

-

Tate says she is glad her young fans can relate to her songs and talk about the things she is going through as a teenager.

-

Tate says she finds it easier to express feelings an opinion through her songs than in real life.

"I can't wrap my head around the situation and form a very strong opinion.

Until I go a write about it, and then I have it. Everything is clear once I write a song about it. "

Tate says that when creating songs lyrics are the number one thing. Also "sometimes ideas will come to me right on the spot, sometimes I have a melody in my head, or sometimes it's all just my subconscious talking."

-

Tate loves writing music as she "can put all of my most vulnerable thoughts out into the world and see who they connect with."

-

If Tate could talk to her younger self she says she would tell herself to stop being a perfectionist and overthinking everything.

"I've always been so scared of messing up, that I've missed out on truly living a lot of moments in my life."

-

Tate said her mind "works a mile a minute"!

-

Tate said on her career: "I always say this, but trust your gut. It's the only thing that you can truly rely on. Your intuition never lies".

-

Tate's first headlining tour sold out. She thought that there would be unsold tickets

"I honestly did not think that anyone was going to show up. I remember asking why we were doing a tour to my managers right before the tickets went on sale. I was like, you realize no one is going to buy tickets right?"

-

Tate is a big fan of actress Zendaya.

"I look up to her so much. From her style to her personality to everything she's ever worked on, I'm obsessed. Not gonna lie, I've watched so many of her interviews and stalk her on Instagram on the daily."

\-

Tate says seeing her face on billboards in Times Square, Madison Square Garden, LA, and Toronto was one of her biggest dreams that came true.

\-

Tate described herself as a VSCO girl! This was a trend on social media where girls used the VSCO editing app to create photos that looked the same for their social media sites.

\-

Tate says her best childhood memory is travelling the world. "I was so lucky to go to so many places at a young age".

\-

Tear Myself Apart is about - according to Tate - how when a relationship falls apart, we tend to blame ourselves.

\-

On Tate's 16th birthday she was in Las Vegas at a dance event. Her friends surprised her at midnight and took her out until 3 am!

-

Tate says that people think she is intimidating and serious because of her music.

But in reality she never sops laughing, and says she is the "clumsiest, dorkiest person ever."

-

Tate started producing music with just a piano. She found that adding more instruments inspired her even more.

-

Tate says that she wants to move to LA when she finishes school as that is where her writers are and it will help her career.

"I think just because the industry is there. It's right there. I've heard LA is crazy at points, and there's a lot of toxic people there, like there's a lot of different personalities. I really want to go there for the work."

-

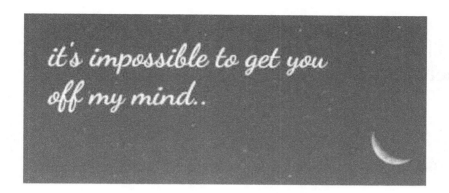

*it's impossible to get you off my mind..*

Tate says an early concert In Amsterdam was "the first crazy fan experience."

-

Tate says with her songwriting she takes a small situation in her life and expands it to make it into a relatable story.

-

Tate says she has been working and travelling since the age of nine. This means she has not had a normal life and it has been difficult to have a regular group of friends.

-

Tate says if she was not working she would be bored.

"I can't go a day without doing something or I will literally drive myself crazy in my own head. It's impossible for me to do nothing."

-

An article said of Tate:

"The path so frequently travelled. The path shrouded in the fickle nature of pop music. But with McRae's work ethic and desire to grow, it is clear she will become a performer who stands out while the others fall away."

-

Tate's star sign is cancer.

Tate said:

"The traits that I actually have from my zodiac sign are that I'm very intuitive and in touch with people's emotions. However, the rest of the characteristics of a Cancer are kind of opposite of me. I do write a lot of emotional lyrics, but I'm not a very sensitive and emotional person. I honestly have a pretty tough skin when you get to know me."

-

Tate is a fan of Dua Lipa."I think her videos are so sick and definitely some of the best I've ever seen. She is for sure one of my biggest idols."

-

Tate is scared of the dark and heights.

-

Tate gets mad about her overuse of the word "like" in her interviews!

-

Tate has never watched any of the Harry Potter films.

-

Spindle said about Tate:

"With a growing fan base, impressive vocals, and relatable music, the talented young star shows no signs of slowing down."

-

Tate wears a necklace her mother gave her for interviews, videos and performances as a good luck charm.

-

Tate only wears bronzer and mascara.

She also couldn't live without lip balm.

-

Tate said on loyalty:

"I would want my fans to know that I am super loyal, and no matter what am always there for people I trust and love. It takes a lot to earn my trust but when it's there, I'll stay there through thick and thin."

-

When Tate was 13 she won a silver medal at the Youth America Grand Prix ballet competition and won a two-week intensive training scholarship at the Berlin State Ballet School.

-

During her audition for the So You Think You Can Dance: The Next Generation TV show in 2016 Paula Abdul was almost in tears after her performance.

-

On Tate's Youtube bio in 2021 she said she was "kinda crazy, kinda chill. I overthink a lot of things, bit of an introvert".

-

Tate's first certification was for her single One Day. It was certified Gold in Canada in April 2020.

-

At the MTV Video Music Awards in August 2020 Tate was one of the nominees for the Push Best New Artist award. She performed You Broke Me First at the pre show.

-

In September 2020 she appeared on the cover of Dork Magazine.

It was her first appearance on the cover of a music magazine.

-

In the late 2010's it was estimated that Tate's average salary as a dancer was $40000.

-

In 2015 Tate won the award for junior Female Best Dancer at the Dance Awards.

The Dance Awards are regarded as the most prestigious awards for dancers aged 5-18.

-

Tate is 5 feet 7 inches (1.7 meters) tall.

-

Tate's eyes are dark brown.

-

In 2020 Tate had around 1.3 million followers on Instagram, 7 thousand followers on Facebook and 22 thousand on Twitter.

-

Tate said that her songs have a songs have a "moodier vibe to them."

-

Tate said she listened to a variety of different music when she was growing up - she was more interested in certain songs rather than a certain artists.

Some favourites were Rihanna, Drake and Justin Bieber.

-

Tate likes to water ski.

-

Tate said the best advice she has been given about her music is to keep evolving, go out of your comfort zone and focus on the process rather than the end result.

-

Her favourite lyric from her EP all the Things I Never said is from Stupid:

"I have a list of all my habits, habits, wish I didn't have it, so bad it's cause all of them are you and the bad things that you do."

-

Tate said in 2020 would be a dream to

collaborate with Khalid or Post Malone. In 2021 she did collaborate with Khalid!

-

In 2017 she created a video series called Create with Tate where she uploaded a new song recorded in her bedroom.

The first song One day got over 30 million views!

The Create with Tate series got Tate a YouTube Artist on the Rise award.

-

In 2020 Tate was named a Vevo DSCVR artist.

This is a list of emerging artists and Vevo arrange live performances for the artists on the list.

-

In 2020, British music magazine NME named Tate as an artist to watch in 2021.

-

A magazine article said of Tate in 2020:

"Personal & Unfiltered, Tate McRae Is The Sort Of Popstar That Will Define This Decade."

-

Tate says that her songwriting is a form of therapy:

"Emptying all my thoughts and emotions onto a piece of paper is how I get over or analyze any situation I have.

I hate talking about myself, so it's my own way of expressing myself through music."

-

Tate studies ballet at School of Alberta Ballet, the training school for the Alberta Ballet Company.

-

Tate's debut album I Used To Think I Could Fly was released on cassette tape.

Compact cassettes were very popular during the 1980s and early 1990s before being replaced by CD's and then streaming. Music cassettes were a great fashion accessory in their heyday and this has led to a cassette revival in the last few years with many artists releasing music on tape.

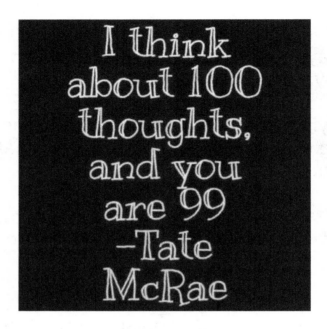

I think about 100 thoughts, and you are 99
-Tate McRae

I Used to Think I Could Fly Tate's first album was released on May 27, 2022.

-

In an interview with American magazine People Tate said that her songs are based in diary entries, especially from ugly thoughts that she has written down.

-

Brady Bickner-Wood from online music journal Pitchfork said of Tate's debut album that it showed she could transcend "online virility".

-

Tate says she does not perform in her home city of Calgary, Canada because "I'm genuinely so terrified to perform in my hometown, just because I know so many people."

-

Tate says that as she has got older and moved into her 20s her taste in music is constantly changing from week to week – from rap music to country music to pop music and so forth.

-

Tate's tour of Oceania in 2022 sold out in four minutes.

-

Tate's debut album was released 10 months after she started to write it.

-

Tate says that she feels she has an old soul and the brain of a 50 year old person.

-

Tate says that when she was writing her debut album she had some famous album producers telling her she was doing it all wrong and that "messed with her head".

She did not know if they wanted to help or manipulate her.

-

Tate had 60 songs to choose from for her debut album. The songs chosen were mostly written by her.

-

Tate says she is quite a private person – apart from writing down her feelings in her song lyrics.

-

Tate says she suffers from impostor syndrome, that she is not supposed to be a famous musician. Sometimes she turns up at a concert venue and thinks no one will show up.

-

Tate says she doesn't feel pressure – she is fuelled by it.

-

It is said Tate is quiet off stage and very talkative on stage. She says she feels free on stage and it is almost as if her alter ego is performing.

-

When producing She's All I Wanna Be 29 mixes were made. Finally a change to a guitar section was made and everyone was happy.

-

Tate says she believes "1000%" in the lyrics she is singing.

-

The title and track listing of Tate's debut album are written in lowercase letters. This trend stems from how people often type using no capital letters on social media and in texts.

-

Tate's favourite lipstick colour? Neutral and a "little bit of pink". Then moisturiser, concealer, mascara and brows.

-

Tate's favourite Taylor Swift songs? All Too Well, You Belong With Me, Love Story and Mr. Perfectly Fine.

-

Tate says she had body issues when she was young as when she was a dancer as a child ballet schools would always be measuring her body.

-

Tate says she has an extroverted persona called Tatiana to help her perform live on stage.

-

Tate says her playlist for long flights includes Billie Eilish, Daniel Caesar, Rex Orange County, The 1975, Jeremy Zucker, Juice WRLD and NF.

-

Tate says her makeup routine is minimalist: "I moisturize my face, and then I just put on concealer, mascara and brows. Then I go on with my day".

-

Tate has said the dance world can be toxic and dancers mistreated. That is why she makes sure her dancers in her shows are treated well.

-

Tate says the song that most summarises her is feel like shit.

-

Tate says that when she meets people for the first time they often say: "No way you write these songs!".

-

Tate says she considered Everybody Wants To Be A Rockstar as the title for her debut album.

-

Tate feels she is  " a level-headed and a pretty normal person who doesn't take things too seriously."

-

Tate says her music is very different from the music of Billie Eilish.

-

Tate marked her 20th birthday with a post on her social media of her sunbathing in a swimsuit drinking Essentia water – which she is sponsored by!

-

Tate says she loves going to Australia, but does not enjoy the jetlag.

-

On June 12, 2022 Tate performed at Wembley Stadium in London for the first time in front of 80000 people at Capital Radio's Summertime Ball.

-

Tate appears in Olivia Rodrigo's video for Bad Idea Right.

\-

The music video for Tate's song with Tiesto 10:35 was filmed at the luxury resort Atlantis The Royal in Dubai.

\-

Tate says she does not write music for specific dance routines in mind.

\-

In 2022 Tate became a brand ambassador for cosmetics company Maybelline.

\-

Tate says the emoji that best describes I Used To Think I Could Fly is a big sad eyes with a smile.

\-

Tate says she enjoys watching cooking shows on tv.

\-

American hip hop artist charlieonnafriday supported Tate on her 2022 ARE WE FLYING TOUR.

-

In 2023 Tate promoted German luxury fashion brand MCM which was her first fashion work. Tate said "I'm a huge fan of MCM. My first bag that I ever got was an MCM bag, and I still wear it to this day. I got it for Christmas, and it's the one object I own that I know I'll keep forever." Tate made a series of music videos wearing MCM clothes.

-

Tate says only in the last few years has she become interested in fashion and developing a personal style. "I want to show myself off and walk into a room feeling confident and show that feminine side to me" she said.

-

Tate says she eats yogurt for breakfast as it is a healthy option.

-

Tate says she always has a part of her outfit that is "weird" such as strange shoes or jewelry.

-

Tate's debut album I Used to Think I Could Fly entered at number thirteen on the US Billboard 200.

-

For a special taste test in 2021 Tate tried pizza flavoured sweets!

-

By the end of 2021 Too Young to Be Sad Tate's EP had over a billion streams on Spotify.

# Discography

## Studio Albums

*I Used to Think I Could Fly*

Released: May 27, 2022

CD, cassette, streaming, digital download

## Extended plays

*All the Things I Never Said*

Released: January 24, 2020

Streaming, digital download

*Too Young to Be Sad*

Released: March 26, 2021

Streaming, digital download

## Singles

*As lead artist*

Non-album singles

## 2017

One Day
Hung Up on You
Hard to Find

## 2018

Teenage Mind
Shoulder to Shoulder
Distant
Can't Get It Out
Drown

## 2019

Slip
Kids Are Alright

*From All the Things I Never Said EP*

Tear Myself Apart
All My Friends Are Fake
Stupid

## 2020

You Broke Me First (Too Young to Be Sad EP)
Vicious(featuring Lil Mosey) (Non-album single)
Don't Be Sad (Non-album single)
Lie to Me(with Ali Gatie)
R U OK

## 2021

Rubberband (Too Young to Be Sad EP)
Slower (Too Young to Be Sad EP)
Bad Ones (Too Young to Be Sad EP)
You (with Regard and Troye Sivan) (Non-album single)

U Love U (with Blackbear)
Working (with Khalid)
That Way"(with Jeremy Zucker)
Feel Like Shit

## 2022

She's All I Wanna Be
Chaotic
What Would You Do
Uh Oh
10:35(with Tiësto)

## 2023

Greedy

*As Featured Artist*

## 2017

All Day All Night (Myles Erlick featuring Tate McRae)

## 2018

Remembering (Yutaka Yamada featuring Tate McRae)

## 2020

Boys Ain't Shit (Remix) (Saygrace featuring Audrey Mika and Tate McRae)

# Quiz

## Quiz 1

1. Where was Tate born?

2. What year was she born in?

3. What was the name of her YouTube song series?

4. What was the name of her first single?

5. Who co-wrote Tate's Song Tear Myself Apart?

6. What does Tate's mother do for a living?

7. Who was featured on Tate's song Vicious?

8. What is Tate's favourite vegetable?

9. What animated series does Tate provide a voice for?

10. How many views has her YouTube channel received?

a: 5 million
b: 100 million
c: over 400 million

11. What is Tate's full name?

12. What does Tate always wear when performing?

13. What is Tate's favorite comfort food?

**Answers on page 80**

# Quiz 2

1. What is the name of Tate's first album?

2. Which country did Tate live in aged 4-7?

3. Who is Tatiana?

4. Does Tate like The 1975?

5. Tate is sponsored by Essentia. What is it?

6. Where was music video for Tate's song with Tiesto 10:35 filmes?

7. Which cosmetics company is Tate an ambassador for?

8. Which song is this lyric from?

"I have a list of all my habits, habits, wish I didn't have it, so bad it's cause all of them are you and the bad things that you do."

9. What colour are Tate's eyes?

10. What was the first single released from Tate's debut album?

11. Which old media format was Tate's first album released on?

## 12. How tall is Tate?

**Answers on page 81**

# Answers to Quiz 1

1. Calgary, Canada
2. 2003
3. Create with Tate
4. One Day
5. Billie Eilish and Finneas O'Connell
6. Dance teacher
7. Lil Mosey
8. Brussels Sprouts
9. Lalaloopsy
10. c: over 400 million
11. Tatum Rosner McRae
12. A necklace given to her by her mother
13. Toast

# Answers to Quiz 2

1. I Used to Think I Could Fly,
2. Oman
3. Tate's extroverted persona she adopts when performing
4. Yes
5. Water
6. Atlantis The Royal in Dubai
7. Maybelline
8. Stupid
9. Brown
10. Feel Like Shit
11. Cassette tape
12. 5 feet 7 inches (1.7 meters)

Printed in the USA
CPSIA information can be obtained
at www.ICGtesting.com
LVHW100721041223
765618LV00004B/93